LUDWIG VAN BEETHOVEN

PIANO TRIO IN C MINOR

OP. 1 / NO. 3

A SCORE FOR
PIANO, CELLO AND VIOLIN

By

LUDWIG VAN BEETHOVEN

WITH A BIOGRAPHY
BY JOSEPH OTTEN

CONTENTS

BEETHOVEN

By Joseph Otten

Born at Bonn, probably on 16 December, 1770; died at Vienna, 26 March, 1827. The date of his birth has never been positively ascertained but is inferred from the fact that the baptismal registry of his parish church gives 17 December as the date of his baptism, and that it is customary in Catholic countries to baptize infants the day following their birth.

Beethoven's father was tenor singer in the court chapel of the Prince-Archbishop of Cologne, where his grandfather, a native of Holland, had for a number of years the post of musical director. He was therefore brought up from his earliest youth in a musical atmosphere. While the father was rigorous and not always reasonable in his rule over the young genius, his mother was often over-lenient with him, a fact which may account for some of the traits of character the young man developed later on.

At the age of five years his father began to instruct him in violin playing, and at eight the musical director, Pfeifer, undertook his training on the piano, while the court organist Van den Eden, and his successor, Christian Gottlob Neefe, instructed him in organ playing, harmony, and composition. As a pianist he made such rapid progress that in a few years he was able to interpret Bach's "Well-tempered Clavichord" and improvise in a masterly fashion. At thirteen years of age he gave forth his first compositions, a set of six sonatas. These and some other productions of his early youth he later repudiated and destroyed. When he was fifteen, Elector Maximilian, whose assistant court organist he had in the meantime become, enabled young Beethoven to visit Vienna. A short sojourn in the imperial city served the good purpose of causing him to realize the incompleteness of his musical as well as his general education. A few years later, in 1792, his patron sent him anew to Vienna with the avowed plan of studying with Joseph Haydn. Instruction under this master did not continue with any system or for any length of time, owing to a radical difference of temperament between the two men.

Beethoven soon found his way to the great contrapuntist, Albrechtsberger, through whose guidance and the private study of J.J. Fux's treatise of theory and counterpoint, "Gradus ad Parnassum", he acquired the solidity and freedom of style which soon commanded the admiration of the musical world. Assiduous study of the works of Handel, Haydn, and Mozart completed what Bach had begun for him in the creative domain. The protection of his patron, the Elector Maximilian, brother of Joseph II, and his striking gifts as player and improvisor served to secure for him, in a comparatively short time, a prominent position in the social and artistic world of Vienna. Archduke Rudolph, afterwards a cardinal, became his pupil and lifelong friend, while numerous music-loving nobles patronized him. As a composer he attracted more and more attention, not only in Austria and Germany but throughout the world. Beethoven's position in life at this time was probably more congenial and agreeable than was that of any contemporary or preceding master. He was enabled to live in comparative ease without the necessity of accepting a fixed engagement or of regularly giving instruction; he was much sought after as an instructor, but he entertained an intense aversion to teaching. His productions of this period, while bearing more and more the stamp of his individuality, yet reflect the influence and manner of his contemporaries, Mozart and Haydn. It was probably more on account of the success of the oratorios of the latter than because he realized the sublimity of the subject that Beethoven undertook the composition of a work in this form, his "Christ on the Mount of Olives". It is well known that in after years he regretted having published it. Especially was he dissatisfied with his treatment of the part of Christ. He had not yet risen to the height of his capacity, or superior to the conventional standard of his superficial surroundings.

When Beethoven was about thirty years old, he contracted a cold which at first impaired his hearing and at length, through neglectful treatment and his careless and irregular manner of living, resulted in almost total deafness. This affliction was destined to have a momentous effect on his life and to determine in a large measure the character of his productions. To be shut off to a great extent from social intercourse, for which, on account of his generous nature, he always had a craving, and to be unable to hear even his own creations, was his painful lot till the end of his days. The isolation and suffering brought about by his infirmity, the deception on the part of people whom he had trusted, and the misconduct of the nephew whom he had adopted, involving him in all kinds of money troubles, caused him to experience periods of depression which almost bordered on despair. Extreme sensitiveness, irritability, and a suspicion of almost everybody he was obliged to have dealing with, added to his increasing misfortunes. General ill health gradually developed into dropsy. In the last stages he was operated on four times without obtaining relief; but through all this time of trial he never ceased composing. Even on his death-bed he sketched a new symphony. He died during a terrific hailstorm after having devoutly received the last sacraments.

Beethoven has left us some 135 works, among them chamber music in every form, 9 symphonies, 1 oratorio, 1 opera, and 2 Masses. Most of these creations must be classed with the greatest music compositions the human mind has produced. In Beethoven, instrumental music, the vehicle of subjectivism *par excellence*, finds its culmination after a gradual development extending over almost three centuries. In his hands it become the most powerful voice of the prevailing *Zeitgeist*. Living in an age and atmosphere of religious liberalism, when Hegelian pantheism pervaded the literature of the day, especially Goethe's fiction and poetry, he could not escape their befogging influence. His statement that "thoroughness and religion are non-debatable questions", indicates both the spirit of the times and his own attitude; it also explains his other saying that "music must strike fire out of the mind of man."

It has been pointed out that in most of his instrumental works no less than in his opera "Fidelio" and the Ninth Symphony, the latter ending with a choral finale on Schiller's "Ode to Joy", Beethoven reveals and depicts the inner struggle against and triumphant victory over doubt. His two Masses bear the same subjective character. They are great works of religious art, but they must be considered apart from liturgical service, to which they do not subordinate themselves. While the first and shorter one in C major, ordered by Prince Esterhazy, does not exceed in length and form what was customary in his day and contains passages of exceptional devotion and beauty, it is still, taken as a whole, too individual and too violent in expression to be admitted for liturgical use. This is true in a far greater degree of his "Missa Solemnis" in D major at the composition of which he laboured for almost two years. This monumental work has been designated as a St. Stephen's Cathedral in tones. Its extreme length and the extensive requirements needed for its adequate performance — orchestra, organ, solo, quartet, and large chorus, together with almost superhuman endurance on the part of the sopranos and tenors — are alone sufficient reasons for excluding it from liturgical service. Performed under proper conditions in the concert hall, it is a mighty profession of faith in a personal God by one of the greatest geniuses of all times, who composed it in the midst of the growing doubt and impending moral and spiritual disintegration of his age.

A BIOGRAPHY FROM
Catholic Encyclopedia, Volume 15, 1913

Drittes Trio.

Dem Fürsten Carl von Lichnowsky gewidmet.

Op. 1. № 3.

Violino.

Violoncello.

Pianoforte.

Var. I.

23

Coda.
Tempo I.

28

29

Trio.

30

Finale.
Prestissimo.

Prestissimo.

34

36

Made in the USA
Las Vegas, NV
02 March 2022

44859579R00026